CW00495620

Mary Potter

Founder of the Little Company of Mary
Her life and vision - and beyond

by
Sr Elizabeth Gilroy LCM

*All booklets are published thanks to the
generous support of the members of the
Catholic Truth Society*

CATHOLIC TRUTH SOCIETY
PUBLISHERS TO THE HOLY SEE

Contents

Acknowledgement

My thanks go to Prof. Tina Beattie from Roehampton University who assisted with the preparation of the manuscript.

Introduction

A Vision

On 9th April 1913 a special English woman died in Rome. Her name was Mary Potter, founder of the Little Company of Mary. Mary Potter would say, "Jesus is my life . . . when I can no longer receive Him, He will come and take me to Himself, and that is what happened. About 6pm on the evening of April 9th, the end came. There was no struggle, no agony."[1]

A few weeks later Mother Cecilia, one of Mary Potter's original five companions recorded having,

"A great feeling that our mother is in Heaven, from a vision I had of her a few weeks after her death. I call it a vision, because it was not dream. What I saw was as follows. I had gone to rest at 9.30 pm and soon fell asleep. There were two windows on the Novitiate floor, one looking north, the other East. I was suddenly awakened by a great noise, which seemed to come from the East window, which was behind my bed. For the moment I imagined it was a shock of earthquake, and I sat up in bed. Then there came, from the East window, Mother, very slowly, as if she were not touching the floor. She came to the middle of the room, just facing my bed. I saw her distinctly. She was all in white, from head to foot; she seemed to be veiled in a robe of transparency and light. Her arms were folded across her breast. I got out of bed and went near to her, to embrace her. I said, "Are you in Heaven Mother"? Then she bowed her head, as if in answer, and a sweet smile lit up her face; with this I went to embrace her, but she faded in my arms, as it were, but I felt so happy in having seen her. In relating this, I speak truthfully . . . I saw Mother. Since then I never feel I want to pray for her, only to her."[2]

Then in 2008

A patient ill in a Little Company of Mary Hospital in the Mid-West of the USA, was experiencing pain and became worried. She also thought she was going to have a panic attack as she felt she could not breathe. She closed her eyes to try to relax and then felt someone (she thought it was a nurse) lift her chin and hold her hand. "I opened my eyes and saw it was a lady dressed like a nun. She had a blue 'cloth' on her head, not black. She was so gentle looking and I felt so safe."

Then she described the soft look in this 'nun's' eyes as if she was "concerned about me". She said she had a beautiful smile and patted my hand. The patient fell asleep until morning. The 'nun' did not say anything to the patient.

Her friend asked her about this 'nun' because she knew there were no sisters on duty that night. Then she asked her if she had heard of Mary Potter. She had never heard of her. So her friend found a picture of Mary Potter and showed it to her. "That's her", she said, and became insistent in knowing all about Mary and her story. "Who is Mary Potter? I would like to know why I was so blessed to see her."

Poverty and religion in Victorian England

If we are to understand what life was like for Mary Potter and her family, we need to situate them in the context of 19th Century England, a society of great poverty and great wealth.

In the poorer areas of London there was no safe drinking water; cholera, typhoid and TB were rampant. On the other hand, the 'wealthy upper class' did not even know about the hardships of the poor.

In 1845 Benjamin Disraeli wrote:

"The English are like two nations, the rich and the poor. They know little of each other's habits, thoughts or feelings. It is as if they live on two different planets."[3]

There were also major changes happening in the Church (the established Church of England and the Roman Catholic Church), as well as in the State and society. This included the passing of the Catholic Emancipation Act of 1829 and the restoration of the

Catholic hierarchy in 1850. Until that time, Catholics had kept the faith by family traditions, in seclusion and through centuries of persecution. The Catholic Emancipation Act allowed Irish potato famine immigrants to have places of worship for the first time, without which they refused to work.

During this time of upheaval, Anglican theologians in Oxford were turning a critical eye on their own church. This was to give rise to the Oxford Movement in 1830s, a movement which grew out of the Whig reforms. It refers to the activities and ideas of an initially small group of young and extremely able Fellows of Oriel College in Oxford, who informally gathered around John Keble, an outspoken critic with regard to the needs and shortcomings of the contemporary church. John Henry Newman led the way by publishing *Tracts for the Times*; John Keble delivered a sermon on 'National Apostasy', then Edward Pusey joined the 'Tractarians' (as they were then called) from Christ Church, Oxford. He taught that the Anglican Church belonged to the wider Catholic (universal) church, and encouraged greater external order and ceremony in services.

There were also complex political questions, such as whether the Church of England was a "department of the Hanoverian State, to be governed by the forces of secular politics, or was it an ordinance of God. Were its pastor's priests of the Catholic Church (as the Prayer Book insisted) or ministers of a Calvinistic sect?"[4]

This was meant to bring about a religious revival, but it succeeded in causing great religious unrest within the Church of England instead. These men were seeking truth and wanted to practise Christianity fully as founded by Christ. They looked to their bishops for guidance, but there was no clarity and no authority on what they were seeking.

From this time, there were many converts to the Catholic Faith, including John Henry Newman, H.W. Wilberforce, H.E. Manning, N.P. Wiseman and many others. This changed the face of the newly restored Roman Catholic Church. Some of the converts to the Roman Catholic Faith following the Oxford Movement influenced Mary Potter later in her life, including Cardinal Wiseman, and Cardinal Manning who were both Archbishops of Westminster.

Then there was the Industrial Revolution and the Crimean War, (1853-56) during which Florence Nightingale awakened the nation to the need for improvement in the care of the sick. There was a great need for the training of nurses, and education would hopefully remove the stigma of this profession. In time, the plight of the sick and those who were dying alone and distressed was brought to the attention of Mary Potter, who was born on 22nd November, 1847.

Early Life

An Absent Father

The history of England in the early 19th Century had a profound effect on the Potter family. The Potters had many problems, mainly to do with religion and money. The family tensions were not helped by Mrs Potter's overbearing nature and Mr Potter's failing business.

Mary Potter's father, William Norwood Potter, was nominally a member of the Church of England, but apparently had no real regard for any religion. He married Mary Anne Martin on 21st February, 1838 in the Anglican Church of St Mary's Newington, in London.

Mrs Potter, a woman who was "full of energy and possessing an indomitable will"[5] was received into the Catholic Church in 1845, shortly before the birth of her fourth child, George. She wanted George and all the other children to be baptized into the Catholic Church and when she told her husband, it caused many distressing arguments. Mr William Potter held the view, (which was generally the custom in those days), that boys should follow the religion of their father; he refused permission. So against his knowledge, Mrs Potter had the children secretly baptized. This was a serious insult to William Potter.

Mary Potter was born in a rented house at 23 Old Jamaica Road in Bermondsey, South London, which was a poor area not far from the docks. Mary was the fifth child, and only girl. Her brothers were William, Thomas, Henry and George. Mrs Potter was suffering from TB during her pregnancy with Mary, which was a great concern for her, as it was well known that full recovery from TB in those days was not common, especially in the lower classes and both mother and child may not survive. Mrs Potter did survive and eventually got better, but as a result, Mary was born with congenital heart disease which left her with frail health for the rest of her life.

Up to this time, William Potter ran a fairly successful pawnbroker and auctioneer business in London, but it started to fail about 1847, the year Mary was born. What with his poor business acumen and losing money after falling into debt, his marriage as well as his business was doomed to failure. It is hard to imagine how sad and belittled he felt.

The discord and lack of trust all became too much for him and he left the family home and never returned. This was about 1848, and he sailed for Australia in July 1850. He remained in contact with his family at first, (presumably he had been sending them funds, as noted in the records of the Bank of South Australia), but this did not continue and soon there was silence from him. Through newspapers and research, it was discovered he married again on the 7th January, 1867. He had two daughters, Hannah Norwood Potter, born 1868 and Kathleen Eleanor Potter, born 1870.

William N. Potter died on 3rd April, 1871 in Blanchetown, Adelaide. His grave was found in the North Road Cemetery in Medindi, Adelaide, South Australia.

His family in England received news of his death by accident, through his obituary in an old scientific magazine. He had been highly respected and liked in his new country.

After his death his son Thomas wrote of him:

"He was a very clever man and in constant correspondence with several learned societies and that is how we first heard of his death. He had already been dead two years before we knew. What estranged him from us all was a question of property for which his brother was trustee on behalf of my mother...He wrote saying that from that day forward, (the date of the letter) we were all of us – wife, children and brother – strangers to him, and he never broke the silence. . ."[6]

A Controlling Mother

As Mary was growing up she developed into a bright teenager who had a personality full of fun and good humour. Occasionally the Potter family entertained the friends of her four brothers and Mary was often asked to

Mary Potter at about 12 years old.

sing and play the piano, as she was a gifted musician and singer.

Mary wrote of her memory of sitting with her mother, "I would sit on the floor with my head in my mother's lap and she, playing with my curls would go on, "And you know, 'Trotty dear', (her family called her this), I was confirmed a few months before you were born and it must have been the Holy Spirit gave you your happy disposition."[7]

Even though Mary was an attractive young woman she was unsophisticated. She captivated people though by her warm manner and good looks. She was fair with a mass of golden curls and her penetrating blue eyes remained her most striking feature to the end of her life.

However, because of Mary's chronic heart disease and constant lung infections, she was often ill. Later on in life, she wrote about this time, saying she bore the pain of bodily suffering and her inner anguish without showing it to others. She would go out for walks with her mother and brothers; listened to their conversations; sang and played the piano for them and mended their clothes. She said she sought comfort from no one.

Looking back over her life, one wonders how much this attempt to cover over her own suffering with a determined attitude of sociability and attractiveness to those around her, would set in motion patterns of interior struggle which would remain a feature of her spirituality.

As the family did not know how much she was suffering, one thinks she may have been taken for granted because of her sunny personality.

Many years later, Mary wrote to her Little Company of Mary Sisters, "Dear sisters, forgive me if I say this again and again, - cultivate a spirit of joy. . . We do see some sorrowful sights and it is a virtue to mourn with those who mourn, but it is wise to look beyond, and we will often find a harvest of glory to God in the patience and generosity of the sufferer."

Mary's education began at home, and her mother was her first teacher. Her 'aunt' Jane Saul then financed her education at Cupola House in Bermondsey, London, where Mary studied music, French language, history, geography, arithmetic, writing and needlework from the time she was 8 years old until she was 18. She attended as a weekly boarder and they were happy years for her. She enjoyed being fussed over by her brothers when she came home, but she was over- protected by her mother and this caused her great anguish as well as real frustration as she got older.

Mrs Potter and Mary moved to Southsea in 1865 because her brother Thomas was transferred to Portsmouth Railway Station as the chief booking clerk. This was a promotion for Thomas and his salary was raised so their rented homes started to improve.

Mary was never left alone with friends of the family, nor was she able to relate naturally to any of her brothers or her own friends because of her mother's overly protective attitude. All she could do was read the books her mother chose for her; play the organ at the Prince George Street Catholic Mission chapel and sing in the choir. Mary was not allowed to have friends of her own, and one wonders how this affected her, as well as a deep sense of loneliness she must have experienced.

A story was recounted many years later about a time when Mary chose to stay behind at the Prince George Street Chapel after Benediction to talk to a young girl. This was Mary Eleanor Smith; even though much younger than Mary Potter, became a close friend. This friend related that when she walked all the way home from church with Mary Potter talking all the way, she was shocked when Mary rang the doorbell which was answered by the maid; her mother was there behind the maid with her watch in her hand. Mary Eleanor said: "I well remember how angry her mother was. She said in a very severe tone of voice, "Mary, why are you so late?" . . . Mary just turned very sweetly to me, without answering her mother, and said "Good evening dear". I was so struck with her meekness and humility, and in my own mind pitied her for having such a hard severe mother. . . Even though Miss Potter still came occasionally to Benediction, I still walked with her, but on reaching her home, I hurried away, fearing her mother's appearance again. . . Mrs Potter was very severe with her only daughter."[8]

There was the enjoyment of musical evenings especially with her wider family, which probably included her grandfather Thomas Martin and her mother's cousins, George and Jane Saul.

The Saul's were wealthy people and generous to Mrs Potter and Mary. They did not have children of their own, and had asked Mrs Potter if they could adopt Mary when she was a baby, knowing the strain Mrs Potter was under, bringing up 5 children without a father, but Mrs Potter would not hear of it. Aunt Saul (as she was called) was an expert photographer and took many photographs of Mrs Potter and Mary. These show Mary and her mother wearing expensive clothes, presumably paid for by Aunt Saul.

Engagement

One particular night, when Mary was 19, her brother Thomas brought a friend home. His name was Godfrey King. He caught Mary's eye and very quickly they became friends. The family were amused when on later visits by Godfrey, Mary prepared for the visit by putting on her best dress.

Even though Godfrey was greatly attracted to Mary, he considered her rather too worldly and he attempted in his own way to help her to be more serious about her life. They enjoyed each other's company and their friendship flourished, though their courtship consisted only in going for (chaperoned) walks, holding hands, strolling along the fields to Goldsmith's farm to watch the peacocks stalking the lawn, or sauntering along the country lanes to Eastney as far as the coastguard cottages in Portsmouth.

Mary wrote in her Autobiographical Notes[9] saying, "I remember, on only one occasion, Godfrey offered me his arm and one of my brothers said, "Mary must be ill to take Godfrey's arm. This was the greatest familiarity which took place between us." After some time Godfrey proposed marriage to Mary, and to the shock of all, she accepted.

During this time, Godfrey introduced Mary to serious theological reading, and as an engagement present gave her some books, among them: *Instructions for Christians of a Timid Conscience who live in the World*. Inside the fly leaf is written: "Mary Potter from Godfrey King, June 1867".

It was through Godfrey that Mary also began to appreciate the beauty of Father Faber's works and the writings of St Grignon de Montfort, whose particular devotion to Our Lady became the basis of Mary's prayer in the future.

Mary wrote in her *Autobiographical Notes*[10] "I used to think how nice it would be to have a little house to ourselves and spend our lives in good works. We could be like Our Lady and St. Joseph." Mary thought this a delightful image and it was only when she spoke about it to Bishop Grant, an old family friend and spiritual guide to Mary and her mother, that he explained the Church would not marry them under those circumstances. He suggested she break off the engagement until she really knew her calling. She was fortunate that Bishop Grant was able to be succinct, yet gentle about the invalidity of such motivation to get married. After being engaged for only four months Mary wrote to Godfrey to terminate the engagement.

Mary's naivety was probably the result of her protected upbringing by her mother and the lack of knowledge about the basics of life. Of course another aspect of her motivation for getting married and leaving home could be that she at least would be free of the pressures of being in a protective cocoon in her home and being dominated by her mother.

Mary felt the break of engagement keenly and Godfrey was devastated and returned to the Potter home many times, asking Mary to reconsider his proposal of marriage. Mary was strong in her resolve not to marry and eventually told her brother Thomas to speak to Godfrey for her.

She wrote many years later that she had "not the slightest regret about her engagement." She said it may be difficult for some to understand how a girl in her teens could be as simple as a little child."[11]

A Time of Discernment

Trying her Vocation in the Religious life

Mary understood then that God had plans for her future and she was open to advice. Even though she had a sense that God was calling her to religious life, she said she really did not wish it herself. She wrote that she loved home life, and dreaded the idea of being a nun with a vague kind of fear. When Bishop Grant, her spiritual friend and advisor, suggested that she look at the possibility of trying her vocation in the religious life, she spoke to her mother about it and together they decided that she should at least go and investigate the possibility.

Mary wrote in her reflections that as she was delicate her mother suggested that Brighton would be a healthy place for her to go, and so they went to seek advice about her vocation at the Sisters of Mercy Convent.

Mary had to obtain a health certificate from a doctor before she was allowed to apply to any convent, because she suffered many illnesses due to her congenital heart condition. If she was not given a medical certificate declaring her healthy enough for religious life, she would not have been accepted into the Convent.

To obtain this certificate, Mary decided to visit her uncle who was a doctor about 70 miles from London in the country. During the visit she wrote, "I did my best to coax my Uncle to write the medical certificate. I played the piano and sang, and indeed saw more life in a few weeks than I would have in years in my own home."[12]

Armed with her medical certificate and a resolve to go and investigate life as a religious, Mary, with her mother and Thomas went to Brighton by train. They arrived on December 7th 1868 and met the sisters. After some discussion the sisters suggested to Mary that the next day, the Feast of the Immaculate Conception would be a good day to receive her as a postulant. This was a hasty decision, and Mary was ill-prepared to enter into religious life with such immediacy. Mary decided to stay, but it must have been difficult to say goodbye for both mother and daughter after such a quick decision. Mary was willing to start in the religious life though, as she felt God was calling her to give herself to Him.

Six months later Mary was received as a Novice in the Sisters of Mercy and her reception was even reported in the local newspaper. It was unusual for local newspapers to report any Catholic activity at all. The restoration of the Catholic hierarchy in England had created considerable anti-Catholic feeling, which had been aggravated and intensified by the numerous conversions following the Oxford Movement. Catholics and Catholic worship were ridiculed and the vigorous "no-Popery" campaign was still in full swing in the press, hence this newspaper article describing the ceremony was most unusual. It recorded that

"On Friday evening the ceremony of receiving a 'postulant' into the religious Order of the Sisters of Mercy was performed at the Roman Catholic church of St John the Baptist adjoining the convent of St Joseph . . . a Miss Potter from London was attired in a rich white bridal dress, a long white lace veil flowing over her from a wreath of white flowers, which rested upon her head; her hair clustering in ringlets around her neck. . . . The Lady Superioress and Assistant . . . led the 'postulant' to the altar, where she knelt and remained upon her knees. The celebrant (Canon Rymer) sprinkled the habit of the Sisters of Mercy with Holy Water which was given to Miss Potter. . ."[13]

During her time with the Sisters of Mercy, Mary was known to have a great spirit of joy and an insatiable desire for perfection. She was introduced to the life of prayer as well as the works of the Order. This special time of learning self-discipline and introducing method into her prayer life had implications for her future. Mary learnt basic teaching skills from the sisters, as well as home care of the sick, the poor and the housebound. She also tried her hand at teaching, but it was discovered that she could not keep the attention of a class of children for any length of time, although she could teach just a few beautifully.

In time it became evident that the life was too demanding physically for Mary and she was advised to leave the convent before her First Profession. Her spiritual director Fr Lambert S.J., who seemed to understand Mary well, was convinced that she should go into a contemplative order that combined Eucharistic adoration and apostolic activity, rather than a strictly contemplative order such as the Carmelites. He wanted her to apply to such an Order when she recovered her health.

When her mother and brother arrived to pick her up on June 23, 1870, Mrs Potter passionately told all those gathered that she would not permit Mary to leave home ever again! This outburst and her treatment of Mary shocked the sisters.

Inner Suffering

On her return home to Southsea Mary's health completely broke down and she was ordered to rest as her congenital heart condition was aggravated by the emotional and spiritual intensity of her time with the Sisters of Mercy. This was the beginning of a period of intense interior trial and pain for Mary. She said she did all she could to recover her strength, as she intended to enter a convent again. Her youngest brother, George, told her, "Remember, Mary, you cannot rest in a hurry, that is one thing you cannot do." Also, not long after her return home, Mary heard that her friend and advisor, Dr

Grant, had died suddenly in Rome a few weeks before she left the convent. She missed him and grieved for her friend. There was no one she could confide in and so she spoke only to God. She knew God was calling her and all she could do was believe. Margaret Silf wrote succinctly, words which poignantly expresses a situation similar to Mary's.

> When my heart is still, God is there beside me
> Silently placing the next stone in front of me,
> Inviting me to take another step across the river.
> Another breath, another prayer, another stone.
> Just one more stone.[14]

Her mother tried to give Mary everything she felt she needed in terms of concern and love, but in fact she smothered Mary with too much kindness. This must have been frustrating for Mary after the independence she had enjoyed in the convent.

Eventually Mary became stronger and was able to visit the mission chapel not far from her home for Mass and Benediction. She also started to visit the lonely, poor and sick in the area and regularly walked around the wharf near the Garrison with her mother and brothers.

One day when they were walking, Mary saw a drunken soldier lurching heavily from one side of the road to the other. As they approached the sentry on guard Mary suddenly realised that if the soldier was seen passing the guard in that condition he would certainly get into trouble and be reported. She quickened her steps and soon caught up with the man, slipping her arm through his and walking along with him chatting away, so that the sentry might think they were simply a soldier and his girl out for a stroll. This sort of spontaneous behaviour upset her family and friends because in Portsmouth there were many prostitutes looking around for soldiers and Mary could have been seen by some as a prostitute, not a kind person trying to save a poor soldier from being put in jail for drunkenness. Her naivety could have given her a bad name! Years later Mary spoke of this incident to the sisters, laughing about it.

People began to carp about her excessive kindness to all and she earned for herself the names 'madcap', and a religious 'fanatic'. Yet the poor seemed to love her and welcome her into their homes. Perhaps we can only guess at the teasing she experienced and the effects this had on her behaviour. On the one hand she seemed motivated, maybe was driven by religious passion and conviction and on the other hand, we knew from her writings that she was experiencing an intense interior struggle, a dark night of the soul.

Prayer for the Dying

It was during this time that Mary's prayer life became more intense and she was given insight into what God was asking of her, even though she felt desolate and had no spiritual support. She was convalescing after another illness from which she felt she would not recover. Mary remembered her feelings of fear, weakness and an inability to pray.

This inner desolation and suffering during her illness was a powerful experience that helped her to realise that so many other people must go through this terrible trial of not being able to pray as well. Mary did not sink into self-pity, as she became aware of this insight but pondered on how she could assist her fellow sufferers.

She spent hours in prayer and reflection before a crucifix; in particular she focused on the Passion and death of Jesus and it was at this time she was drawn to pray for the dying. She started to think of the possibility of founding in the Church a group of religious Sisters dedicated to the spiritual, and, where possible, the physical assistance of those who were sick and dying. By1872 she became more and more convinced that this is what God was asking her to do. She wrote in her *Autobiographical Notes*, "When I was praying there was a Presence – I saw nothing and yet Our Lord Crucified seemed present for a few instants."

Who would help her to understand the Graces God was sending her? So much was happening within her and she knew God was asking more of her. She needed to speak to a priest, but whom?

Spiritual Guidance with Monsignor Virtue

By this time in the Southsea district, Catholics were rejoicing in the arrival of a priest, Monsignor John Virtue, the recently appointed Military Chaplain of the Portsmouth Garrison. He did not live in the Garrison but in a private residence in Ashburton St, Southsea where he had a small chapel. Mary heard that he invited people to his home for Mass and Confession, and it was not far from her own home. So she joined that small group and asked him for spiritual guidance in the area of her new devotion, her spiritual life and her desire to re-enter a convent. Monsignor Virtue agreed to accompany Mary in her spiritual journey.

Up to this point, Mary did not have anyone to share her deep spiritual insights. Certainly she was friends with her parish priest, Fr Horan, but she felt shy in expressing her spiritual experiences out loud, so she wrote many letters to Monsignor Virtue prior to her visits to him on Saturdays and when she went to confession they discussed the content of her letters.

These letters (unfortunately none of which were dated),[15] are important and have provided a unique insight into the spiritual journey of Mary and the journey of the birthing of the vision she had for the Little Company of Mary. Mary always considered these letters she had written to Monsignor Virtue to be the most important ever to be written by her. As Monsignor Virtue chose to reply to them through the confessional we have a one way conversation only, and any responses that Monsignor Virtue made are in Mary's references to them in her letters.

Mary wrote years later in Rome in her *Autobiographical Notes* that she asked Monsignor Virtue to return these letters to her, to show another confessor, (Fr Selley) and he told her he would destroy them, but he finally wrote to her saying that he sent them to Cardinal Simeoni at Propaganda Fide Archives in Rome where they are today. The Little Company of Mary sisters now have copies of all the letters, something that Mary was not allowed. Mary knew these letters were important and she later wrote to Fr Selley that they "show so clearly that this matter is God's work, not mine".[16]

A crucial insight came to Mary during this period. She was reading a book that she thought would help her and make a difference to her spiritual life called *Treatise on True Devotion to the Blessed Virgin*, which was translated from the French by Fr F Faber in 1862. This book, written by St. Grignon de Montfort was not easy to read and Mary was unimpressed with the difficult language and put it down. Not to be daunted, she decided other eminent and knowledgeable people vouched for it, so she read it again and again, and prayed for the grace to understand it; to receive the message she felt God was giving her through it. Eventually the impact of the message of this book gave Mary a focus and a passion to follow God in a way that changed her life. As St Grignon de Montfort says so clearly in his book, we are to offer all our actions, prayers and sacrifices to Jesus through Mary.

She wrote to Monsignor Virtue about this devotion and found out that he "disapproved of True Devotion saying it was almost condemned by the church."[17] She mentioned in her letter to him that she was confused by his attitude because later he told her it was approved by the church.

Because this devotion made such a profound difference to her life and focus, and because Monsignor Virtue was so negative about this devotion, Mary continued to ask him what he meant. "You made me very unhappy and I do think you might look through the book again, for I feel quite sure you have not read it through. Will you please do that, because how can I be easy when I know you have not read the book?"[18]

This honesty and directness on the part of Mary may have disturbed Monsignor Virtue. Women did not usually challenge priests about their theology. It seems Mary was so focused on God and her insights were so clear, that her directness was a grace, rather than anything else.

She started to live her days in the 'Spirit of Mary' and consecrated herself entirely and forever to Christ through the hands of His Blessed Mother on the 8th December 1872. The daily living of this consecration would be the secret of Mary's spiritual progress from that day forward.

Mary wanted to write her own commentary on de Montfort's book under the title, *The Path of Mary*. It was completed in September 1875, but due to the opposition of Mgr Virtue, it was not published until twelve months later, and then anonymously. In this book, Mary Potter writes, "What then is this seemingly new devotion you naturally ask, and the answer may be given in few words. It is the devotion practised by Our Lord Himself. . . Here is what I would have you to do. Make, after a fitting preparation . . . an entire consecration to Mary of all the spiritual and temporal possessions you have, or may have in the future."[19]

A Broken Heart

Even though she respected and obeyed Monsignor Virtue, she struggled within herself about his advice and attitude. It was a fraught relationship and Mary felt Monsignor Virtue did not understand or accept the inspirations God was giving her.

She wrote to him about her awareness of the need to pray for the dying. *"I cannot but feel I have had a call from God to devote myself to help save souls in their last hour. . . I have been drawn so strongly to pray for the dying and I believe it to be a work appointed for me, perpetual prayer for the dying"*.

Monsignor Virtue did not reply to this insight and during their next meeting Mary challenged him by saying, *"you do not speak to me of what I have told you, but I must ask you to do so now. I feel I am preparing for some great grace to be given me, the Holy Spirit, the Gift of God."*

Mary also shared with Monsignor Virtue that she felt a new Religious Order, having Calvary as its model, was needed in the Church and of her increasing awareness of a call to "help save souls in their last hour". Monsignor Virtue was then quick to refute this, telling Mary not to think she had been given a revelation. His admonitions to pay less attention to her prayer life and more to the ordinary business of daily life became stronger as Mary began to relate experiences that she claimed were direct communications from God. Monsignor Virtue was convinced that Mary was 'delusional' and told her so. This must have hurt Mary deeply; still these insights were significant enough to draw her to a new sense of herself, and to an independence of spiritual thought and action.

One wonders why Monsignor Virtue reacted in this way. One thought was perhaps there was a general wariness about women, having mystical experiences. Women in general were seen as second class citizens in any walk of life particularly in the Victorian era; but women who questioned priests and discussed God with any insight were not accepted at all. Mary Potter was no exception, particularly someone who was only 27 or 28 years old. To make matters worse, Mary shared with Monsignor Virtue that she now felt she lived in an inner union with Jesus and Mary. This sense of unity, she informed him, was accompanied by feeling *"united to the Most Holy Trinity in an unspeakable way... being joined in wonderful union with the All Holy God and feeling that it was His will that you should be one with him."*

Monsignor Virtue was unimpressed by this disclosure. He was even less impressed with Mary's belief that God *"had given me a great grace, which led me to believe he would have the Precious Blood specially honoured."* He was dismissive of the claim. Not only was he dismissive, he was horrified and told her to "stop prophesying", cut down on her prayer and under pain of mortal sin, stop entertaining such blasphemous and ridiculous thoughts. He told her that her 'Inspirations' were 'Delusions' brought to consciousness by what he appears to have considered a pious but neurotic mind.

All this affected Mary deeply. In her Autobiographical Notes Mary wrote, "During this time of sorrow, I had only occasionally bodily suffering. At times I would think it would be a relief if my body was in pain, it might distract me from the fearful anguish of soul which I bore without showing and did my few duties, going out, singing and playing the piano. I had hours to myself in the day and used to come down from my room as if nothing was going on within me. I sought comfort from no one, confided in no one. When my confessor told me it was a mortal sin to believe in these inspirations, which God permitted, it pierced my soul in the most painful manner possible."[20]

Mary continued to write to Monsignor Virtue knowing that each time she suggested something he would pour cold water over it. Towards the end of 1875, Mary Potter wrote in her letter to Monsignor Virtue, "You broke my heart. You may tell me I am deluding myself, but God is renewing every grace within me and giving me his peace that it seems can never be taken from me . . . My own heart has seemed ready to break, but Our Lady helped me so that I could ask God to ease me."

Mary had many mystical experiences during this time and she wrote at length about them. One such experience was when she heard a voice saying to her, "It is my will that you should do this work," and again, "I have chosen you, and my question "Why to me?" and the answer, "the weak things of this world and the poor."[21] Mary said she just knelt and prayed, she knew not for how long.

In Mary's last letter to Monsignor Virtue she wrote "If you ever wish to make up for what you did not of course intend, but which nevertheless, without exaggeration, you broke my heart, when what you said to me made me think and feel almost as though I was already in hell . . . [and], if ever you have to say such things to anyone else, mollify it, encourage them at the same time, for it is dangerous."

Mary realised that Monsignor Virtue's continued criticism and negative responses were simply not helpful and indeed were positively dangerous for her. In January 1876 Mary terminated the relationship. "This will be the last letter I think I shall trouble you with, at any rate for a long time." Mary continued on to explain to him just how much pain his counsel has caused her.

On the other hand, Monsignor Virtue, through causing this suffering, brought out in Mary a mature confidence in God, and received insights that only God can give. These sufferings she endured was gift to the Little Company of Mary, because Mary understood the great graces given to her and at the same time accepted her unworthiness in receiving such graces. She handed onto her sisters this understanding through her writings and her personal example.

Father Selley

Mary then wrote to a Father Selley a Marist priest who was recommended to Mary through her friend, Mary Fulker. Mary was not asking him to direct her, but simply she was "in hope of obtaining a friend for a work now in its infancy." She told Father Selley her experiences and her desire to found an Order devoted to praying for the dying, its spirit and model being Calvary.

Father Selley's reply to Mary enthusiastically approved her plans and said he had great confidence that Almighty God was calling her to accomplish a great work and to supply a great need. He wrote, "You may rest assured that you shall have all my help, first by my prayers and commemorations at Mass and secondly by furnishing you with postulants". Fr Selley supported Mary Potter in the time ahead, and for this he suffered rejection and criticism from the Bishops and his Superiors.

Vitality and Strength of Vision

Mary's profound love of the church and loyalty to those in authority did not make her docile, because the Will of God was at stake. The letters Mary wrote to Monsignor Virtue and to Fr Selley convey an image of God, and Mary's devout spirituality. In all this we must not lose sight of Mary's vitality, determination and strength to follow the voice of God. Mary's clarity of vision was coming together and she became stronger and more determined to follow this call.

This brought criticism from her mother, her brothers, priests and bishops. Fr Selley was informed that any co-operation he might give Mary in founding an Order would be considered as deliberate disobedience both to Dr Danell of Southwark and to the Cardinal Archbishop of Westminster.

What was noted by so many was Mary's great calmness and resignation to these rejections and in a letter she writes to Father Selley: "I was neither surprised nor disturbed at the contents of your letter. . . Please do not blame either Dr Danell or His Eminence. They are both so good. I only see Almighty God's Will in what they do. . . ."

Mary also became more aware of the 'Maternal' love of God. In her later writing, Mary spoke to the sisters about being 'mothers'. "You must be true mothers, mothers by suffering, even unto death. Offer your life to give birth to children in the spirit of the Mother-like Shepherd who tells us 'I lay down my life for my sheep'. "[22]

In the 20th and 21st Century, theologians have explored the maternal aspect of God, and we find in Mary Potter and many of the medieval mystics a strong sense of the Motherhood of God. Again and again we see in the life of Mary Potter the great vision of theologians of today. After Mary founded the Little Company of Mary, she wrote to all the Popes until her death asking them to proclaim Mary as "Mother of the Church". This did not happen though until 1964 when on November 21st Pope Paul V1 proclaimed Mary as "Mother of the Church". This declaration took place at the closing of the Third Session of Vatican II.

Mary Potter's many writings over the span of her life were Mariological and those who read them are directed toward a relationship with Mary, and as quoted so much by de Montfort, devotion to Mary is "To Jesus through Mary." Mary Potter's theology therefore was bound in Christology as well as Mariology.

In the light of this Christological and powerful image of Calvary - Mary at the foot of the Cross - Mary Potter became more and more aware that it was imperative that an Order was founded to pray for the dying, to be with others, as Mary was with her Son as he was dying.

She was suffering terribly by now, physically as well as emotionally as there were so many who rejected her and turned away from her. She was asked by one of the women who were thinking of joining Mary in this new venture in what way was she suffering. In a letter of 1st December, 1876 Mary told Sr Magdalen Bryan of her physical sufferings, which were serious, and dismissed them by saying, "I do not say much about bodily suffering. There are doubtless numbers who are suffering more. . . Do not think I am unhappy or have lost my peace. Not at all, I am cheerful and happy." But what Mary regarded as bronchial trouble was, in reality a malignant breast cancer. Mary wrote that she looked upon the pain of the loss of a Confessor, (Father Selley) as infinitely more trying to bear.

Escape to Nottingham

By this time, Mary's brothers realised that she was in fact not a fanatic, or mad, but close to God. They were sorry they made it so difficult for her and ended up helping her in any way they could. Mary's youngest brother, George, now a teacher at Radcliff College in the diocese of Nottingham, wrote to Mary suggesting that she should apply to Bishop Bagshawe (the Bishop of Nottingham) for permission to work in his diocese. George said he would consult the Bishop about the matter. The Bishop agreed with George and told him to send Mary to him to speak about allowing her to commence her work in his diocese.

Before she set out, Mary really wanted her mother's blessing because she loved her, and even though Mary was 28 years old and did not need her mother's permission to leave, she still tried to reason with her. She did all in her power to win her mother's approval but Mary could not convince her that this work was really God's Will. Mrs Potter remained hostile to all her arguments and refused to give her blessing.

Still feeling somewhat uncertain about leaving, Mary had not made arrangements to go to Nottingham. Then one day in January, 1877, Mary agreed to a trip to Brighton for the day with Marguerite, her beloved sister-in-law to visit Marguerite's nephew. When it was time to return to Southsea and were waiting on the platform for the train, Mary suddenly remembered the Gospel of the day, the story of the *Finding in the Temple*. She stood there and started to pray. Marguerite stood with her, wondering what was happening as Mary was attracting attention to herself by blessing herself repeatedly.

Mary Potter and her beloved sister-in-law, Marguerite, wife of Thomas Potter unknowingly became the first *Little Company of Mary* Associate.

Suddenly Mary described a great peace that came over her. She made up her mind and quickly decided to go to London instead of going back to Portsmouth. Marguerite of course was distressed at the thought of facing her mother-in-law and her fury, yet she felt compelled to help Mary, as she was not only her sister-in-law, she was her friend. Marguerite promised to look after her mother and to take Mary's place at home. Marguerite emptied her pockets of the money she had and handed it over to Mary to pay the fare to London. When Mrs Potter was told by Marguerite what Mary did, she was so angry that she did not speak to Mary for 18 months.

Mary caught the London train and stayed the night with her brother, Henry who, the next day, arranged and paid for her journey to Nottingham; as the train was leaving, he thoughtfully pressed ten shillings into her hand. Just before 8pm on Saturday, 13th January, Mary reached Nottingham station. She went straight to St Barnabas Cathedral where she arranged an interview for the next morning with Bishop Bagshawe. Mary rented a room in Derby Road near the Cathedral in readiness for her interview with the Bishop. What was she feeling? She could imagine the fury of her mother with Marguerite and the distress it caused the household. On the other hand, she knew she must just go and do what was right.

The next morning Mary knocked at the door of the Bishop's house and Bishop Bagshawe gave her a cordial

First Convent in Hyson Green, Nottingham, an old stocking factory which Mary Potter herself made habitable for the first sisters.

welcome to his diocese. He was shocked though to see a 'lay woman' and not a Religious Sister! Bishop Bagshawe was a socially minded man, and he recovered enough to accept her. He needed help in his Diocese and he was not going to turn away a willing person to assist with these great needs. He arranged for her to remain in Nottingham with a Catholic family until something could be settled for the beginnings of her 'special work'. Then he suggested that Mary go and find a cheap place which he offered to pay the rent for 12 months so they could begin.

Mary went to a poor area called Hyson Green about two miles from the Cathedral and found an old disused stocking factory in Lenten Street. It was a mess, and Mary discovered there were no staircases; rooms filled with rubbish of every description and it looked like the village rubbish heap. Yet, in spite of this, Mary was satisfied the building could be repaired. Workmen invaded the house and the repair was soon making good progress.

Then one by one the small group that Fr Selley had encouraged from St Anne's in Spitalfields in London came to Nottingham. In a letter Mary wrote to one of the first companions she said, "I do not wish to make a grand start, for probably it would be a grand failure."

While all this was happening, Mary commenced visiting the poor and sick in their homes and soon became a well-known figure around Hyson Green. She met many people who lived in dire poverty neglecting their faith and their prayer. She helped families in their homes. Some of those she visited had children to feed, housework to do and to cook for their husbands. They were too ill to do any of this and Mary got on and cared for the sick, cleaned the house and cooked a meal when needed.

The date of the opening ceremony was set for Easter Monday, 2nd April, 1877. So popular had Mary and her companions become because of their involvement with the poor and sick that many people came to the opening. Catholics as well as Protestants assisted as well offering crockery, evergreens for decoration and food parcels. One Protestant man lent a fine organ which proved invaluable.

The Bishop and his assistants arrived and he dedicated the convent to the Maternal Heart of Mary. They had an impressive sung Mass, with help from the Children of Mary from the Cathedral. After Mass the Blessed Sacrament was exposed until evening. It was a great day of rejoicing for the little group just starting out.

Shortly after the opening, Mary Eleanor Smith, (Sr Cecilia) a young woman of 18 who had known Mary since she was 9 years old, joined Mary and Mrs Elizabeth Bryan (Sr Magdalen) and then some time later, Edith Coleridge joined them. She had trained as a nurse at St George's Hospital, London and was a welcome addition, particularly as she was the only member with any scientific knowledge of nursing.

The question arose: What were they to call the new group? Mary, after a lot of discussion with Fr Selley and others, wanted to call the group the *Little Company of Mary*. She surprised everyone by her insistence on it. The bishop approved, and he said later to Fr Selley, "I think she had light on the matter and the best right to settle it." Eventually they also settled on a simple dress of a plain habit of black with a pale blue veil.

The first reception of the habit ceremony took place on the 2nd July, 1877. Bishop Bagshawe gave the habit to Mary and her five companions, Magdalen, Agnes, Cecilia Philip and Joseph. The chapel was crowded and the people gathered outside to see the five new Sisters with the blue veils! Mother Cecilia wrote about this wonderful ceremony some years later said in her reflections. "We had all been working hard up to the time of the ceremony, and there had not been a chance of getting anything to eat. Afterwards when all were gone and we said our prayers and retired to rest, dear Mother Mary appeared with a tray and glasses of egg flip and tiny cakes. Here was the first loving act to us after receiving the habit. Poor Mother must have been tired, but there was nothing selfish in her noble loving soul."

Little Company of Mary

The Little Company of Mary had commenced. Mary and the sisters went out and helped the sick and poor in their homes. Mary took the inexperienced sisters out with her to care for the sick and dying and showed them how to care for them practically. There was a story that Sister Cecilia Smith relates when she has just arrived in Hyson Green. Mother was showing her around the village to make the acquaintance of a lot of the poor and sick. Cecilia wrote,

"Mother had with her food for the poorest and a big apron which she put on and began our first district nursing. I looked on in amazement; I knew Mother was frail, but her love for the poor made her strong. Once, on our rounds with Mother, we had just arrived in a very poor alley, when a woman met us and said, 'For God's sake, Sisters, do go to Mrs. N. she is suffering so much, she will be glad to see you.' We went up one flight of stairs, where we found a young woman weeping with a newborn infant crying. The woman said the baby was too weak to draw milk from her and would surely die from starvation. Neighbours had said, 'Why not get a breast pump'? But, she said, it cost too much and her husband was only a poor labouring man." Cecilia wrote, "I was only 18 and stood listening, but Mother went to work, first rubbing, very gently the engorged breasts and then to my astonishment, she bent down and sucked that poor woman's breasts, till the milk came. The baby was put at once to its fount of life and both mother and child were happy and contented. I looked at Mother in wonderment."

Another time Cecilia remembered, was a Sunday evening,

"and usually compline was sung by our village choir, followed by a sermon and Benediction. There were about 8 or 9 of us sisters at the back of the Chapel, and about 50 people in front. On one particular Sunday evening, just as the sermon commenced, loud heavy steps sounded on our staircase and who should appear, but William E.- a good hardworking man, but who, occasionally, took 'a drop too much'. This time he had taken a good many 'drops' for as soon as the sermon started, William began to talk very loudly. The priest turned to Mr Tacey who looked after the chapel, and said, 'Take that man out'. There was silence for a moment, but when William was approached, he became very loud and abusive and would not go. Then Mother went and spoke kindly to him, and Mr Tacey said, 'I'll take him home Mother Mary'. But at this William scowled and said to Mr Tacey, 'Don't you dare lay a hand on me', and then turning to Mother, 'I'll go with she,' and went away like a lamb with Mother who took him down the lane to his cottage and returned in time for Benediction".

The Meddling Bishop

"As a community we were happy and united at first", wrote Sister Cecilia, "but the Bishop began to send us postulants, some of whom were most undesirable, one in particular was a Mrs Frances White". According to Sisters reflections she was "a widow, already well known in Nottingham, and an extremely aggravating person, about 50 years old. Before she was even given the Habit, the Bishop appointed her as the bursar. . . 'Dear Mother was treated as a fool by her' remembered Sister Cecilia.

As Mary was the only one in the community who understood religious life, having completed her novitiate with the Sisters of Mercy, she tried to teach these sisters about living life in community. The rest of the group had no idea about this and Mary's instructions were seen as superfluities, but Mary saw them as essentials. These inexperienced women saw the Little Company of Mary as a pious society with very little in common with other congregations.

Bishop Bagshawe did not agree with Mary Potter's vision of the Little Company of Mary, and could not understand that she wanted the sisters to be both 'active and contemplative'. He also could not understand that Mary's inspiration was for the sisters to be on Calvary with Mary, with constant prayer for the dying an essential part of their lives.

So the Bishop sent his delegate to tell Mary that he had appointed Mother Magdalen Bryan as Superior, and Mary was deposed. This was just two weeks after the formal clothing. Not only was she deposed, she was also told not to speak to the sisters.

Mary lived in the community continuing to set the tone by her lived example of prayer, gentleness, and a non-judgemental attitude. Then some months later the Bishop appointed Mary as 'Mistress of Novices', but, she still could not speak to the sisters, (especially about their personal spiritual life). She was only allowed to give a spiritual talk to them once a week. Mary, seeing the great dangers in these restrictions went to express her views to Bishop Bagshawe. He did not take any notice of what Mary was saying and kept to his decision that she was to do no more than explain the nature of True Devotion and the spirit of the Little Company of Mary to the whole Community.

Mary felt that training the Novices like this was an impossible task and an 'uphill work'. Then she wrote, "It is permitted by God for some purpose. I offer it to save poor dying sinners. If I cannot do the good I would for those who should be my own here, I must pray that I may do more good for the souls of those I do not know." Sr Philip (a strong woman), was so upset about this injustice that she stormed to the Cathedral to complain to the Bishop. All he said was that he wanted to "crush her" to try her, and she 'passed the test'. The Bishop was known to 'try' people, against all other advice. He later admitted how wrong he was to do this.

Even through these terrible trials, Mary took the opportunity to write. She was a gifted writer and wrote many books, unpublished conferences and letters. During this time when Mary was not allowed to speak to the Novices or the sisters, she wrote a book on the Spirit and Charism of the Little Company of Mary and it was to prove invaluable to the Order. This book is called, *Mary's Conferences to her Loving Children both in the world and in the Cloister* which was published in 1878.

The funds of the convent were low, so Mother Mary who was not well and Sr Cecilia were sent out to beg for money. They were away for about four weeks and they did not raise much money for the community. On their return they had to report to the postulant-bursar, (Francis White, the widow who had just entered). She did not hesitate to insult them when she considered the takings insufficient. As time went on Sr Francis became cruel to the sisters, particularly if they were ill. She even confused Bishop Bagshawe by her behaviour. The Bishop did not understand the chaos that was happening and did not help in any way.

The pain and suffering within the community from inappropriate people entering, and the interference of Bishop Bagshawe could have closed the whole community down. Mary Potter knew however that it was not her idea to found the Congregation; it was a direct Grace from God. Therefore somehow Grace would prevail. Mary remembered many years before when she was suffering after she left the Sisters of Mercy of a special insight she received. In this insight she wrote in her *Autobiographical Notes*:

"The Little Company of Mary is a direct impress from the Most High. God visited my room with a series of marvels, and simple as I was, unread in mystical theology or even ordinary writings upon direction, I still knew that God's Manifestations to me meant something great, something indeed of moment."[23]

Mary knew that it was not her work, so she was calm, because she understood the power of listening to God's will.

Mary Potter and Cancer

Mary, as we know was never in good health, but in early 1878 she began to feel great pain in one of her breasts. Nothing was done about this as Sister Francis White, who was acting as the superior of the community, refused to accept that Mother was ill. Toward the end of the year, the local doctor diagnosed a malignant breast tumour and ordered an immediate Mastectomy (removal of her breast). Preparations were made for the operation and it was performed on the kitchen table in the convent on 8th December. They used little anaesthetic because of Mary's congenital heart condition. When Dr Hatherley told her this Mary said, "I do not mind pain." She was semi-conscious during the whole procedure but at one stage said to Dr Hatherley, "Oh, Doctor, I can feel you cutting me." The sisters who witnessed the operation were horrified at the pain Mother was experiencing, and six months later Mother's other breast was removed under the same conditions because of the cancer. Sister Cecilia wrote that all those present were greatly impressed by Mother's sweetness and tranquillity under these painful conditions.

Her recovery was slow, and again Sister Francis was very hard on Mary as she was convalescing and sent her out to beg only a short time after the operation which nearly killed her. The sisters could not take any more and complained bitterly to the Bishop.

He listened to them at last and ordered an election on February 12th, 1879. Mary Potter was elected and re-instated as Superior of the community. The Bishop was dismayed that Sister Francis was not elected, and punished the community by withdrawing his financial support. It did not take Mary long to sort out the difficulties of the community and dismiss unsuitable candidates and sisters, so the religious spirit could once again reign and a commitment to the vision be maintained. Even though there were still many deep and unusual problems caused by the Bishop, Mary's deep faith never faltered.

Journey to Rome

There was still inappropriate expansion of the sisters to parishes and the persistent crippling interference by Bishop Bagshawe, so much so that Mary felt the community would completely disintegrate. She then decided to apply to go to Rome and seek papal approbation. This meant that the status of the Community would change and instead of the community being ruled by the Local Bishop, they would be under the Vatican. Mary also wanted to obtain a Blessing and approval of her rule from the Holy Father.

At first the Bishop would not give his permission, but eventually he said yes, "How could I refuse the request of a dying woman" he said, thinking Mary would not live long. The Bishop provided letters of introduction to various prelates and priests. On September 24th, 1882, Mother Mary, Mother Philip Coleridge and Mother Cecilia Smith travelled to Rome. Mary Potter's family provided the funds for the journey.

Pope Leo XIII

On the long journey to Rome, Mary suffered two heart attacks and was very ill. Mother Philip was distressed and Mother Cecilia was frightened that Mother would die. On arrival in Rome, the group were introduced to a Monsignor Luigi Macchi at the Vatican. He was warm and welcoming to the sisters and invited them to join a

French group which was to be received in a public audience by Pope Leo XIII the following day. The Audience was in the Holy Father's private chapel. Mother met the Holy Father and knelt at his feet. She asked him to bless the Little Company of Mary and the Rule and then she would return to England. "But" said His Holiness, "Perche? Why not remain? The gates of Rome are wide open to you."

With the help of their new friend Monsignor Macchi, they planned what they would do and where to live. Word got around that there were "English Sisters" in Rome and they were able to give comfort and nurse the sick and the dying in their homes and thus they gained a reputation for quality care. There was an outbreak of Typhus in the seminaries and the Cardinal Vicar of Rome was petitioned to give permission for the sisters to nurse the students. This was recorded as the first time a woman was to enter the all male dominion of the Roman Colleges!

Mary had an extraordinary gift of knowing when someone had died. Mother Cecilia wrote in her reflections "that on two occasions, at least, Mother knew of the death of persons who had died at a distance and before the news could reach her in the ordinary way. It first happened the same month in which we arrived in Rome, October 1882. During the night (we had to share a room) the sisters heard a noise, like someone falling, and Mother Philip called out, 'What is that?' Mother Cecilia wrote, Mother beckoned to me, (putting her finger on her lips) to go to her. Then she said, 'Pray for Father T.N. . . he has gone to Our Lord.'" Mother Cecilia continued in her reflections, "We had not heard of him for months before we left England, and did not know of any sickness regarding him. However Mother was right in her knowledge of his death, for after a week, a letter came from England, saying Father T.N. had had an accident and died immediately, giving the exact hour of his death, which was the hour in which Mother told me he had gone to Our Lord.

The second occasion that I knew of was at the death of a very kind friend from our early days in Rome, Monsignor James Campbell, former Rector of the Scots College, who died at San Girolamo, Fiesole (not far from Florence). He had endured many months of suffering, mental as well as physical. Mother knew he was going through a great personal trial in Rome, and invited him to go to the community in Fiesole as a guest of the Little Company of Mary. He accepted the invitation and went. He never returned to Rome. On the evening of February 16th 1902, during our recreation, Mother sent a message to the Novitiate, asking the Novices to make the 'Stations of the Cross' for Monsignor Campbell. I was a little surprised at this order, but of course, all went at once to the Chapel. This was exactly at 8.15 p.m. Nothing more was said about the matter. After midnight

Mary Potter's tomb, St Barnabas Cathedral, Nottingham. In 1997 Mary Potter's remains were translated from Rome to Nottingham, the cradle of the Little Company of Mary.

a telegram came, which read 'Monsignor Campbell passed away peacefully at 8.15pm.' On reading this, I immediately remembered the occurrence of the previous evening. Next morning I asked Mother, 'Did you know Monsignor Campbell was dead?' 'Oh, yes,' she answered, 'I saw him just there, (pointing to a corner of her room), as one sees things like this, and he looked very peaceful and happy, and had his hand raised in blessing.' It seems he died a most peaceful death, exactly at 8.15pm on February 16th, 1902."

Another occasion, during Mother's last illness in April 1913, her good friend, Cardinal Respighi died. The sisters fearing the news would be too severe a blow for Mary, tried to hide it from her. In the evening one of them had to answer her question, "When did Cardinal Respighi die?"

Expansion of the Little Company of Mary

As time went by, and Mother and the sisters became more known, their work increased. Mother sent for more sisters from Hyson Green, and eventually they were able to be sent to Florence and other areas where they were needed. They changed houses as the group increased. Even though nursing seemed to be the great need at the time, Mary Potter was determined that the sisters not get caught up only in one area and also not neglect their prayer life for the dying. In the *Rule of 1886*, it stated that the sisters "will also undertake other spiritual and temporal works of mercy when there is any occasion for doing so…"

Through the contacts of many Bishops and Laity, the Little Company of Mary was becoming well known. There were invitations to go to other countries as the ministry the sister's were doing was appreciated.

Mary Potter was cautious, and did not get caught up in spreading the group too thinly. There was a request in 1884 from the new Archbishop of Sydney in Australia for the sisters to start a foundation. Mother spoke to Archbishop Moran, but told him she was not ready to send the sisters so far away at that point. The Order was still technically a diocesan congregation. Mary wrote to

Bishop Bagshawe and he gave his approval. Still Mary was uncertain, so she said no.

The following year, Archbishop Moran was back in Rome to be made a Cardinal. Again he approached Mary to send sisters to Australia. This time she said yes! So in 1885 the sisters prepared to sail to Sydney. Mary was concerned that there be no interference to the Spirit and Charism of the Little Company of Mary and had the foresight to ask the Cardinal to write a letter to the College of Propaganda: "Promising that no attempt would ever be made to separate from its present stem in Europe, the Little Company of Mary, whom he had offered to plant in that part of the Church." The Little Company of Mary then spread to the Southern Hemisphere and flourished, attending the sick, the poor and the dying where there were needed.

In 1885 Count Arthur Moore of Tipperary, Ireland, was in Rome and his wife became ill. She was nursed by the sisters and his wife was impressed by their care of her. The Count made a vow that if his wife recovered he would try and establish a branch of the Little Company of Mary in Ireland. After many discussions, the foundation of the Little Company of Mary was eventually made in Limerick and six sisters commenced at St John's Hospital on 10th October, 1888.

There were many more foundations, and this was a crucial time of maintaining unity within the Little

Company of Mary. The sisters sent out were young; many had not made their Perpetual Profession. Mary was a risk taker and she trusted the sisters to live out the Spirit and Charism to all they ministered to.

Building a hospital in Rome

In Rome Mary saw the need to build a hospital for the many patients that needed care. This was a mammoth task and a risky one, especially in a foreign country. After many years of struggling and arguing with builders and architects, Mary at last saw the completion of a 'Crucifix' shaped building not far from St John Lateran, in Via S Stefano Rotondo, called Calvary Hospital. It was here in 1908 that the first Training School for nurses commenced in Italy.

Death of Mary Potter

Gradually Mary's health weakened and she began to have great difficulty with her vision as well. The sister's became alarmed. One day Mary handed Mother Cecilia an envelope on which was written in Mary's own handwriting, "My Wishes;" it was her Will. She explained to Mother Cecilia, "After my death poor Mother Philip will be so upset that she may not remember where these papers are, and it is better for you to know." Mother Cecilia said: "Mother, what are we going to do when you die?" Mary said, "I shall come back again," and then you will not feel so lonely." Signor Carletti knows where he has left a place for me in the crypt."

Eventually news had spread around Rome that "La Santa Madre" was seriously ill and many people called to see her before she died. The doctor said he regretted that she was suffering so much and that there was little he could do to relieve the terrible pain, she assured him, "I have always wished to suffer for Our Lord and I would not want to be without pain now." Later in the day, Cardinal Merry del Val, Secretary of State, sent the special Blessing of Pope Pius X.

As we began with the story of her death and remembering the oft-repeated words: "The day that I can no longer receive Our Lord in Holy Communion, Our Lord Himself will come to take me," we end the story as Mary begins the journey of dying. Mass was being celebrated in her room and at the Consecration she stretched out her arms suddenly, uttering the Holy Name repeatedly and then went unconscious. After some time and after receiving the Last Blessing, Mary Potter uttered a cry and then peacefully died. It was 6.15 p.m on Wednesday 9th April, 1913. So we finish, but this is only the beginning.

Mary was buried in the cemetery of the Campo Verano and then as she promised, her body was transferred to the Mother House at San Stefano Rotondo on the Coelian Hill on the 26th April, 1917.In 1988, Pope John Paul II declared Mother Mary Potter 'Venerable', the first step to canonization. The more we read and understand the depth of the courage, vitality and sanctity of Mary Potter, the more we realise how much more there is to know. What she accomplished in her life, particularly in the light of her frailty, physical pain and terrible opposition from people, even those closest to her, is in fact a miracle in itself. Her inspirational example of calmness and peace in the light of these sufferings is something only those who reflect carefully would understand.

Mary only saw God's Will, and she was always so happy to do that. As one priest said when she died, "Mary did one thing only, she loved God."

Returning Home to England

In 1997 Mary's body returned to England. She now rests in the Cathedral of St Barnabas, Nottingham; the cradle of the Little Company of Mary. Many people pray there for courage and strength. She remains the 'heart' and 'hearth' of the Little Company of Mary, an example of perseverance in time of suffering and of a joyful and loving woman.

Little Company of Mary in the 20th and 21st Century

Where does the heart of this unique spirituality of the Little Company of Mary lead us today? Reflecting back over 130 years since the foundation of the Little Company of Mary, it's mission and ministry has touched thousands of people. Mary Potter was so concerned about social justice, right relationships with our Creator and with each other that she wanted her sisters to *"Go where you are needed"*. If this need was an obscure part of a poor city or another country, *go* there: if a person was lonely: *be* there. The sisters have been asked to bring the Mother Love of God to everyone in need.

Throughout the world there have been many communities of Little Company of Mary sisters, working where they were needed, in hospitals, parishes, counselling, and many other ministries. Mary Potter did not want the sisters to have just one prime ministry, because that would stifle the gift. She wanted the sisters to be aware that people were dying everywhere; dying physically, spiritually, emotionally and psychologically. She wanted the sisters to be alert and listen to the needs of the time, and be flexible to these needs. She wanted them to stand with and be with the suffering.

Here are some stories that will give a good example of 'listening to the needs of the times' today.

Korea

Following the Korean War in the late 1950's the country was devastated and the people suffered from poverty, and many illnesses. The Bishop in Kung Neung, east of Seoul was so frustrated because of the lack of finance, support, food and medical help for the people, that he asked the Little Company of Mary Sisters in Australia for help to set up a clinic. Initially two sisters were sent, and then followed another three sisters, followed by many more. The sisters of course went to language school to help them in their ministry and then a clinic was built and the sisters treated many hundreds of people who had TB, malnutrition and many other diseases. In time they commenced the first hospice movement in Korea. Today, there are many Korean Little Company of Mary Sisters looking after the sick, the dying, caring for children, and the poor.

Albania

In 1992 the new Papal Nuncio in Albania, who knew of the sisters' work in Malta, wrote inviting them to assist with medical care for the suffering in Albania. They were just freed of 40 years of communism, with resulting poverty, poor services of any kind and a lethargic uncertainty of where to begin to restore the country. In

1993 Little Company of Mary sisters arrived in Korce, (SE Albania) from the UK and was soon inundated with many calls for nursing care.

It was decided to build a clinic which would be for the Albanian people. It was opened on 7th October, 1996. It thrived quickly, but sadly and unexpectedly anarchy, due to the collapse of a government run pyramid insurance scheme necessitated the sister's return home.

After 7 months three sisters from England returned to Albania – the clinic was now just a shell and there were insufficient resources to repair and open its doors again. Care of the dying in their homes remained the focus of their ministry and they were blessed with two Albanian nurses who became committed to palliative care.

After varied and careful training outside Albania with one doctor, the nurses assumed management of the clinic and the sisters then withdrew in 2004. The Sisters in the UK continue to financially support the clinic and visit twice yearly to give support and look at new initiatives. The clinic has greatly developed into a 'Centre of Excellence' of palliative care with the Albanian management, in ways which could not have happened whilst it was run by foreigners.

This is mission, and mission is about empowering people to be the best they can be and give them a sense of independence and dignity.

Zimbabwe and South Africa

Mary Potter wanted the Little Company of Mary to be in Africa as she knew the need was so great. Such was her vision of the world. The sisters went to South Africa (Port Elizabeth), in 1904, and then to 'Rhodesia', (today called Zimbabwe) in 1938. The sisters are still in Zimbabwe and South Africa, ministering among the people and have cared for the sick and dying faithfully for many years.

When the apartheid system was defeated, the people in South Africa thought the situation of the people in the 'shanty towns' would improve but it has not, and we are told 'apartheid' is still happening there. It seems the only help they get is through people who call on the consciences of the world. One such person is Sister Ethel Normoyle an Irish Little Company of Mary Sister sent on mission to Africa. In 1988 she visited a settlement just out of Port Elizabeth and saw the plight of over 130,000 people. They have no electricity or water, (there are 13 taps to cover the 130,000 people) and unemployment is rife. Large numbers of the population also suffer from HIV/AIDS.

Sister Ethel set up a school and basic clinic under a tree in Missionvale. She is a great communicator, and contacted a group of concerned business leaders who visited the area. This resulted in the building of 3 small rooms for the school and clinic near the 'tree'. Since then Sister Ethel has organised the setting up of a large care centre which includes a fully equipped clinic, nutrition unit, a library and offices. Even Queen Elizabeth II visited Sister Ethel in Missionvale in 1995. Since then there has been the opening of classrooms in the primary school, a home based care initiative and other projects directly focused on HIV/AIDS pandemic. She launched a carpentry unit and planned a new resource centre including a hospice. A church was built, a clothing centre; vegetable gardens for the people to grow their own vegetables; a skills centre and many other ways to help give the people back their dignity and respect. It is the passion and great compassion of sisters and lay people that enabled all this to happen. They have taken the spirit and charism of the Little Company of Mary to those in need just as Mary Potter directed her sisters to do.

As the great *Nelson Mandela* once said.

"Poverty is not natural . . . and overcoming it is not a gesture of charity – it is an act of justice."

Internationality of the Little Company of Mary

The story of need is worldwide. Mary Potter saw this in her day, and today the needs are no less. The world is in turmoil and people are dying, the spirituality for mission is as important as ever.

In the vision for the future, the Congregational Leadership of the Little Company of Mary have set up an International Novitiate which is in Manila, Philippines.

The Little Company of Mary faces the situation of growth of vocations in the East and Africa, and a lack of vocations in the West.

Little Company of Mary Associates

Again, Mary Potter wanted lay people to be more involved in making a commitment to praying for the dying and have involvement in the prayer life of the sisters. These lay men and women are called LCM Associates. They are those lay men and women who have made a commitment to the Little Company of Mary spirituality and vision. They are led through a programme, and make a commitment to pray for the Dying and further the Mission of the Church through the Little Company of Mary charism. Their commitment is renewed each year.

Mary Potter had such vision from the early days of the foundation of the LCM in involving the Laity. She knew that laity and Religious sisters work well together in their different vocations.

Little Company of Mary Affiliates

Little Company of Mary Affiliates are those who pray for the dying each day and have made a commitment to join with the sisters in their ministry of praying for the dying of the world in union with Mary on Calvary.

The Greater Company of Mary

There is a vast number of persons who are involved in the ministry and life of the Little Company of Mary; co-workers, colleagues, volunteers, families of sisters, friends of any religious affiliation or denomination. Without these people, the Little Company of Mary would not be as effective in their ministries.

Mary Potter Volunteers

Mary Potter Volunteers are members of the Greater Company of Mary who share in the Little Company of Mary mission and ministry to the suffering and dying people of our world. The 'MPVs' have a specified period of commitment to active ministry, helping where they are needed. During ministry placement, a member of Mary Potter Volunteers is assigned to a Little Company of Mary community for regular sharing of ministry experience. This helps to ensure a mutuality of mission/ministry support for both volunteer and the community.

From the early days in the life of the Little Company of Mary, Mary Potter envisioned that women and men from various walks of life would volunteer their talents and gifts to enrich the mission and ministry of the Little Company of Mary. In turn, they themselves would be enriched by the spirit of the Congregation.

The Maternal heart

One young woman was discerning her vocation in life and was overwhelmed by the many Orders she encountered. She admired the Sisters who taught her; and met many other sisters in her search. The one Order that stood out to her was the Little Company of Mary. Why? She said there was nothing big or spontaneous in the meeting, but when she got to know the sisters she discovered a real humanity, common sense and compassion. They seemed to be people who listened. She described it as a 'maternal' feeling. She felt close to God when she met these sisters. It was right.

Later she learnt about the 'maternal' aspect of the Little Company of Mary. The mission of bringing the compassionate 'mother love of God', as demonstrated by the love of Jesus dying on the Cross and the 'mother love of Mary' standing at the foot of the Cross to a world suffering in so many diverse ways, bringing hope into a world where hope seems dead.

For this young woman it became clear that the Spirituality of the Little Company of Mary was what she was looking for. She felt a 'burning' within her heart. She *knew* she was being called by God.

She felt a call similar to that of the sickly young woman from a dysfunctional family who had a vision, borne of faith and vitality and sustained by commitment, a vision that still fulfils a need today and makes her a possible saint for the 21st Century.

Mary Potter wrote so succinctly in *The Path of Mary*,

"Who remained faithful, even in the most terrible hour of the Crucifixion? Who did not abandon their Lord, when even He seemed to be abandoned by His Heavenly Father? Who hoped and trusted in Him, when others despaired? Who, though weeping, adored and loved, whilst others scoffed and mocked? Who were they, and where did their strength come from, to stand in the face of the Passion? Consider the answer well. Those who remained in the company of Mary"[24]

The *Constitutions of the Little Company of Mary* state:

". . . It is at the foot of the Cross that we take our stand with Mary, are truly her companions and enter more fully into her Maternal Heart."

This is the heart of the Little Company of Mary that Venerable Mary Potter founded in 1877.

Prayer for the Beatification of Venerable Mary Potter

O God to whose glory the Little Company of Mary was founded by Venerable Mary Potter, grant that she may be beatified soon so that her work and spirit may benefit still more the suffering members of Jesus Christ. Amen

Mary, Mother of the Church may this ardent apostle of your Maternal Heart be more widely known by special favours granted through her intercession. Amen.

For favours received or further information, write to:

Little Company of Mary Generalate
28 Trinity Crescent
Tooting Bec
London SW17 7AE UK

Endnotes

1 *Unpublished Reflections of Mother M Cecilia Smith LCM*, p. 12, one of the original five members of the Little Company of Mary. Her personal reflections commenced during a Retreat at St Girolamo, Little Company of Mary Community in Fiesole, Italy, August 1902 and continued until after Mother Mary Potter's death in 1913. Little Company of Mary Archives, Tooting Bec, London.

2 *Mother M Cecilia Smith LCM* Personal Reminiscences p. 13.

3 Benjamin Disraeli, *Sybil or The Two Nations*, Chapter 5, book 11, pg 68-69. Leipzig, Bernh, Tauchnitz. June 1845.

4 *Pusey House: St Giles, Oxford.*
http://www.puseyhouse.org.uk/house/history/oxfordmovement
The Oxford Movement, 4th August, 2009.

5 E. Healy *Mother Mary Potter*, Sheed and Ward (London, 1936), p. 22.

6 Eve Healy, *Mother Mary Potter*. P. 22.

7 M. Potter, *Autobiographical Notes*, p. 1, Reflections written in obedience to her Director, Father J. Ryan SJ, 1902, during a Retreat at St. Girolamo, Little Company of Mary Community, Fiesole, Italy. Little Company of Mary Archives, Tooting Bec, London.

8 Mother M. Cecilia Smith. *Personal Reminiscence*, 1902 P.1.

9 M. Potter, *Autobiographical Notes*, p. 3.

10 M. Potter, *Autobiographical Notes*, p. 3.

11 M. Potter, *Autobiographical Notes*. P. 3.

12 M. Potter, *Autobiographical Notes*. P.7.

[13] Eve Healey, *Mary Potter*. London 1936. Sheed & Ward.

[14] Ref. Margaret Silf, Landmarks, *An Ignatian Journey*, Darton, Longman & Todd. 1998. pg 164-165 Used with permission of Author.

[15] *M. Potter, Letters to Monsignor John Virtue.* November 1874-May 1876 (From photographs of the originals in the Archives of the Sacred Congregation of Propaganda Fide, Rome).

[16] Letters of Mary Potter to Father Edward Selley SM 1876-1882. Letter no. 2.

[17] Virtue Letters, no. 2.

[18] Virtue Letters, no. 2.

[19] M. Potter, *The Path of Mary*. 1878. LCM Chicago 6th edition.

[20] M. Potter, *Autobiographical Notes*. P.10, 1870-1876.

[21] Virtue Letters, no. 3.

[22] M. Potter, *Mary's Conferences*, p. 19.

[23] M. Potter, *Autobiographical Notes*, p.

[24] M. Potter, *The Path of Mary*. Chapter 1, P.18.

Bibliography

Dougherty, P. *Mother Mary Potter*. Portia Press Limited, Whitchurch, Hampshire. Great Britain. 1961.

Healy, E. *The Life of Mary Potter*. Founder of the Little Company of Mary. Sheed & Ward. London, 1936.

Potter, M. *The Path of Mary* Published 1878. 6th Edition LCM Chicago USA.

Potter, M. *Mary's Conferences*. Published by Little Company of Mary, Kogarah. NSW Australia. 1988 Edition

Silf, Margaret. *Landmarks. An Ignatian Journey*. Darton Longman & Todd, 1998.

West, E.A. *One Woman's Journey*. Mary Potter, Founder Little Company of Mary. Spectrum Publications, Australia. 2000

Some Prayers for the Dying

Loving Father, by your boundless love for every person.
Have mercy on the dying.

Compassionate God, by the love you have for Mary, the Mother of your son Jesus.
Pardon the sins committed in life by those who are now dying.

Loving God, through the intercession of Mary your Mother.
***May the dying be strengthened by your gifts of hope,
courage and peace.***

Jesus, by your redeeming love,
Bring the dying to fullness of life.

Jesus, by the love you have for the heart of your Mother.
Have pity on the dying.
Maternal Heart of Mary, more loving and suffering than the hearts of all mothers.
Implore God's mercy for the dying.